CLASSICAL GUITAR CHRISTMAS
Collection

ISBN 978-0-634-03336-0

HAL•LEONARD®
CORPORATION

7777 W. BLUEMOUND RD. P.O. BOX 13819 MILWAUKEE, WI 53213

Visit Hal Leonard Online at
www.halleonard.com

CLASSICAL GUITAR CHRISTMAS
Collection

Page	Title
4	ANGELS WE HAVE HEARD ON HIGH
6	AULD LANG SYNE
8	AVE MARIA
10	AWAY IN A MANGER
11	CANON IN D
18	DECK THE HALL
19	THE FIRST NOËL
22	GOD REST YE MERRY, GENTLEMEN
23	GOOD KING WENCESLAS
24	HARK! THE HERALD ANGELS SING
26	HERE WE COME A-WASSAILING
27	I SAW THREE SHIPS
28	IT CAME UPON THE MIDNIGHT CLEAR
30	JESU, JOY OF MAN'S DESIRING
36	JINGLE BELLS
35	JOY TO THE WORLD
38	MARCH
41	O CHRISTMAS TREE
42	O HOLY NIGHT
45	O LITTLE TOWN OF BETHLEHEM
46	SHEEP MAY SAFELY GRAZE
48	SILENT NIGHT
50	WE THREE KINGS OF ORIENT ARE
54	WE WISH YOU A MERRY CHRISTMAS
52	WHAT CHILD IS THIS?

Angels We Have Heard on High

Traditional French Carol

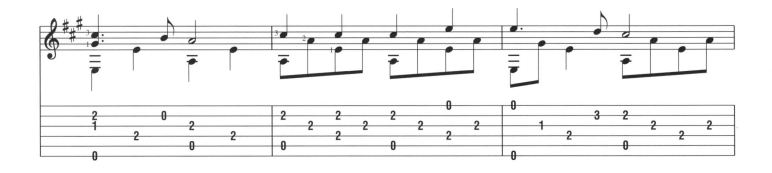

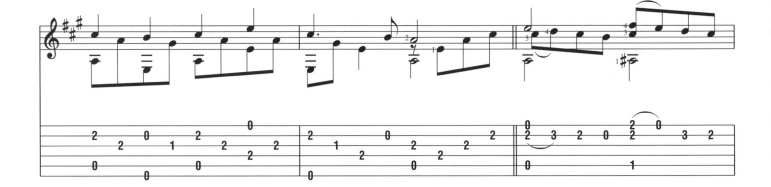

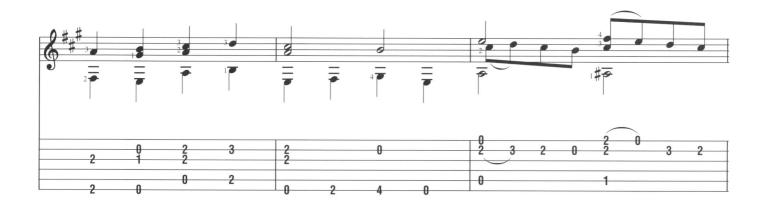

Auld Lang Syne

Traditional Scottish Melody

Drop D tuning:
(low to high) D–A–D–G–B–E

Moderately

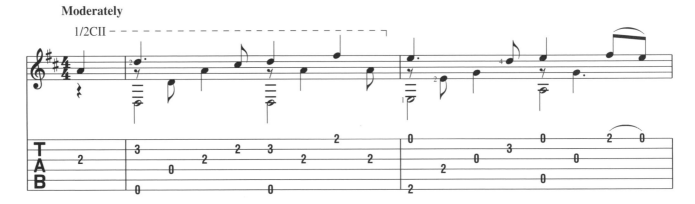

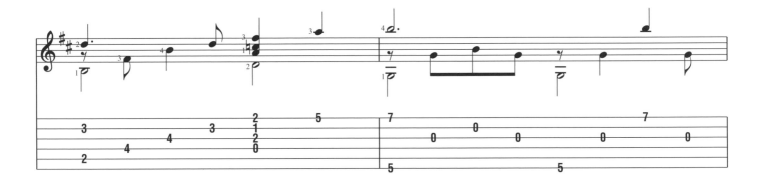

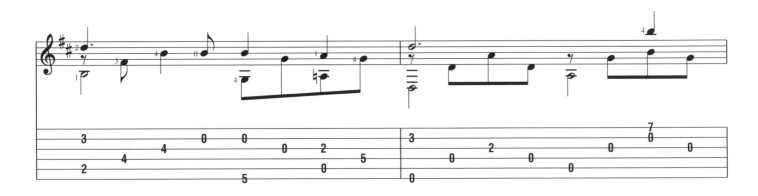

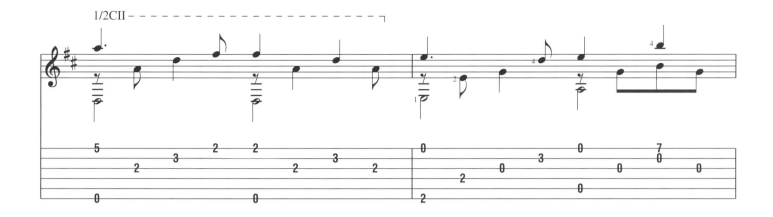

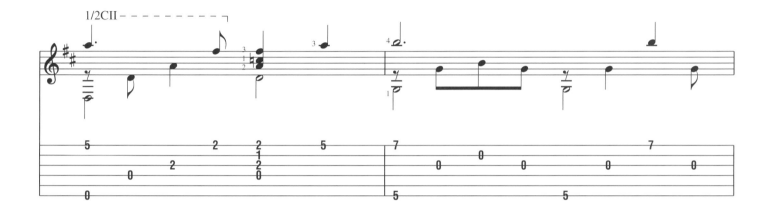

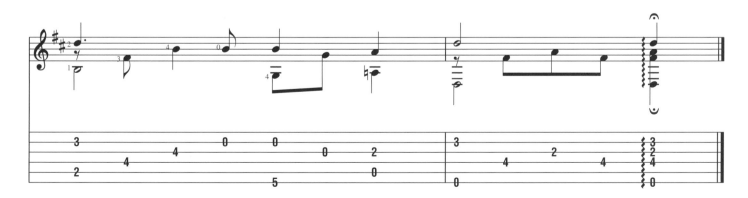

Ave Maria

By Franz Schubert

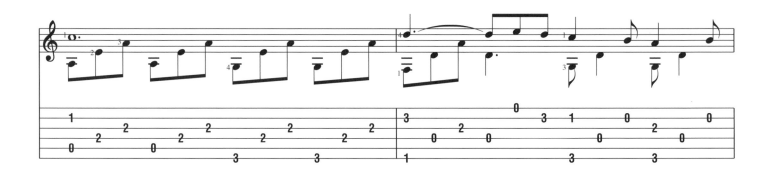

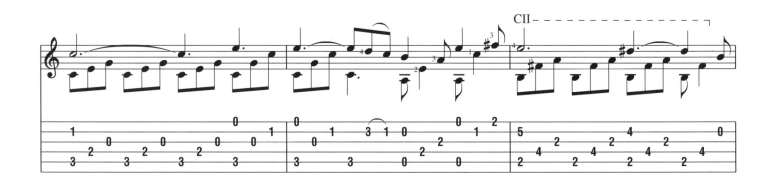

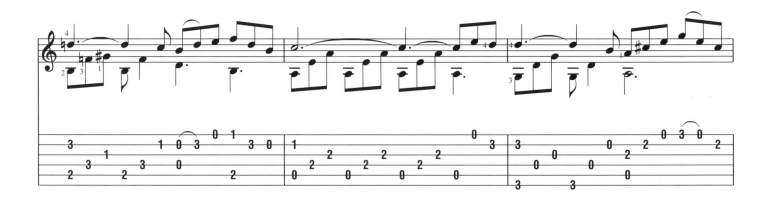

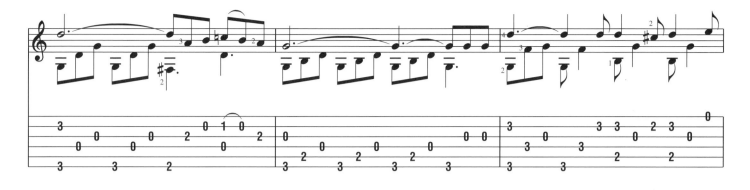

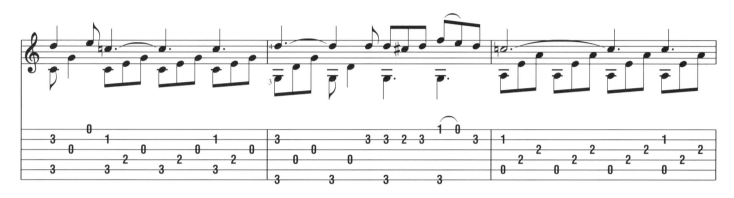

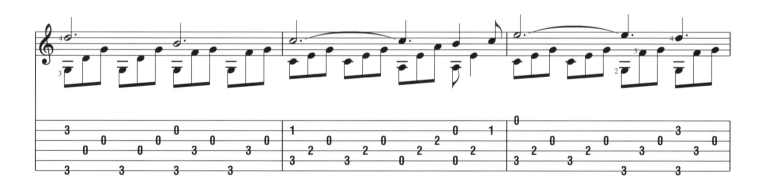

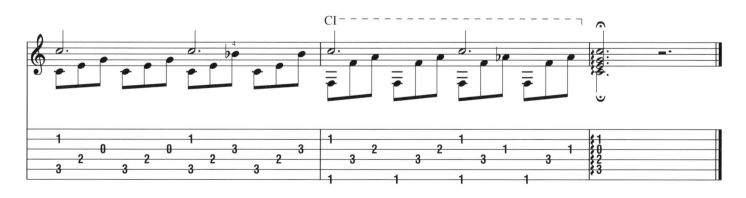

Away in a Manger

Music by Jonathan E. Spillman

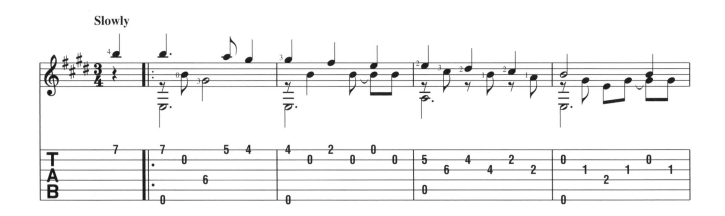

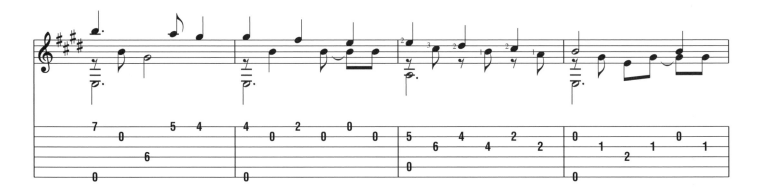

Canon in D

By Johann Pachelbel

Drop D tuning:
(low to high) D–A–D–G–B–E

Moderately

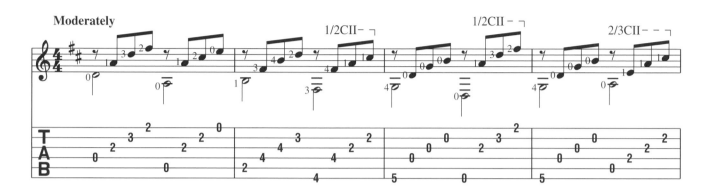

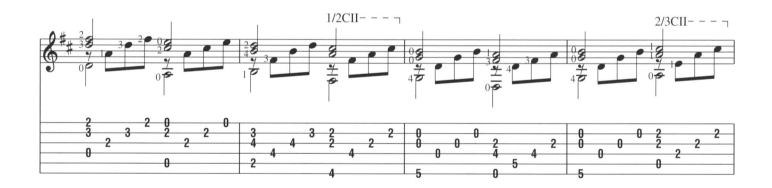

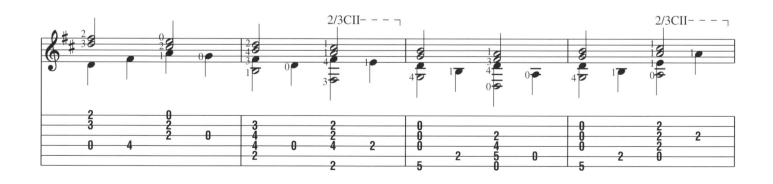

11

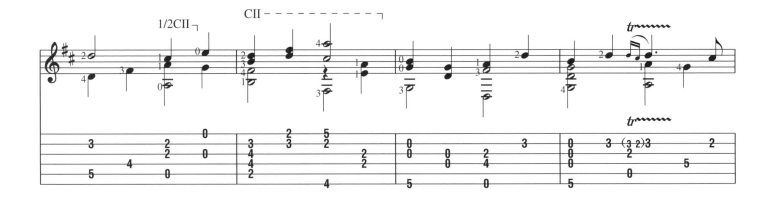

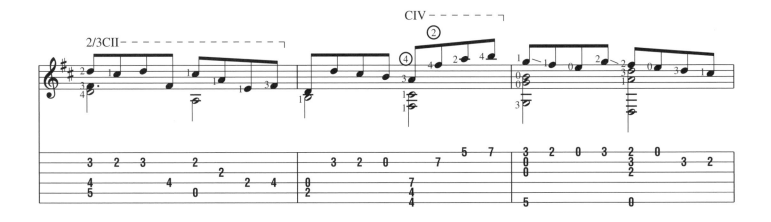

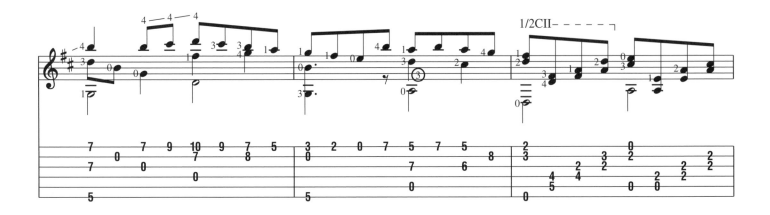

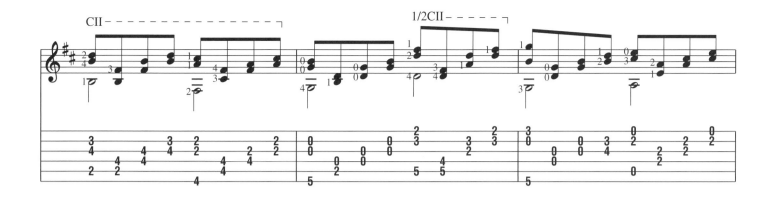

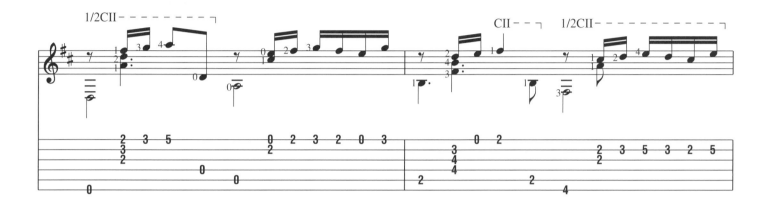

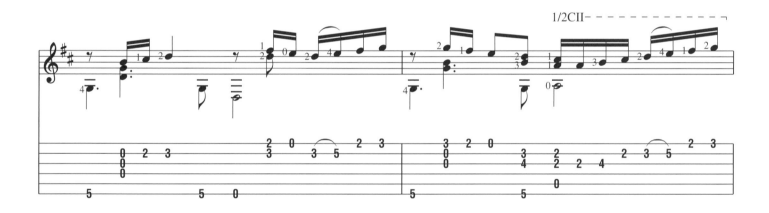

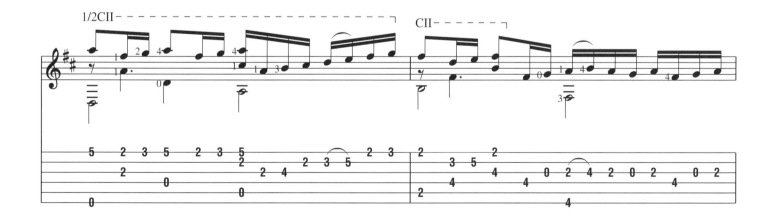

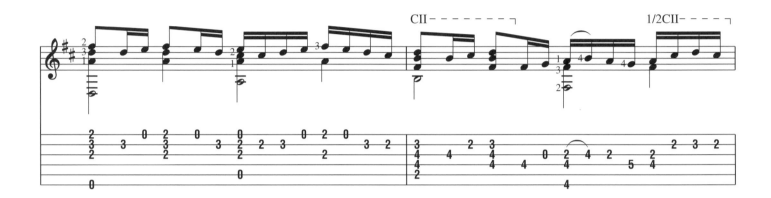

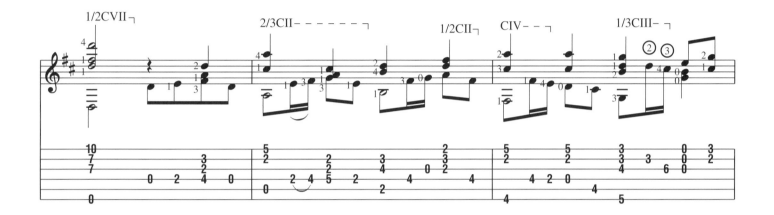

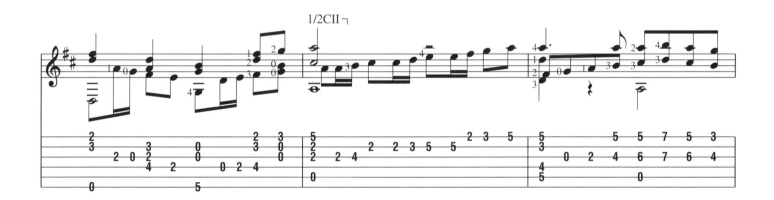

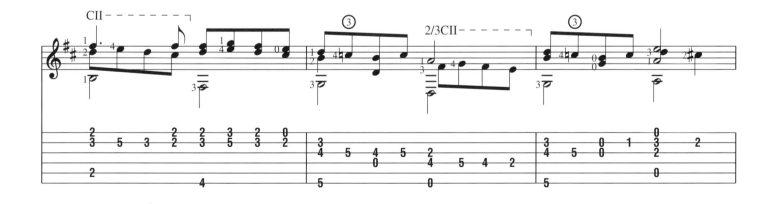

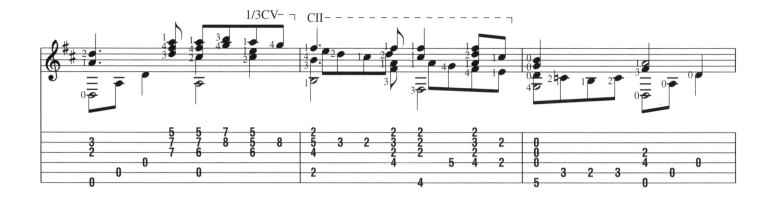

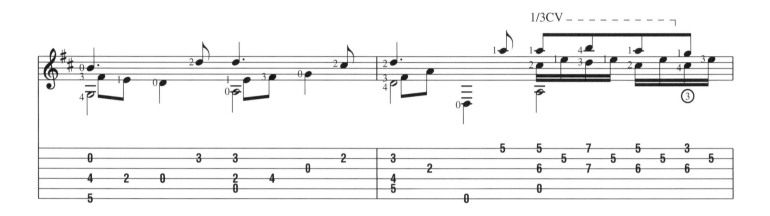

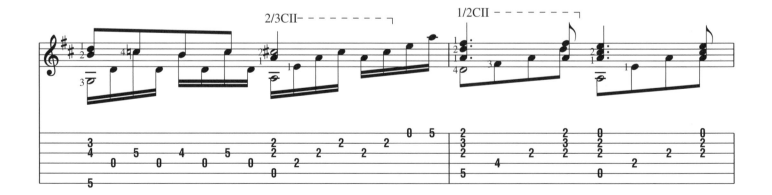

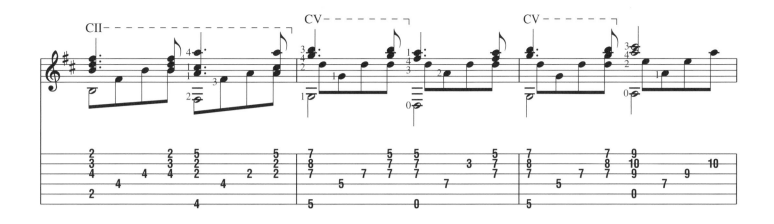

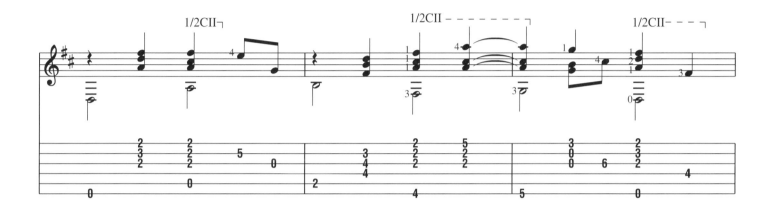

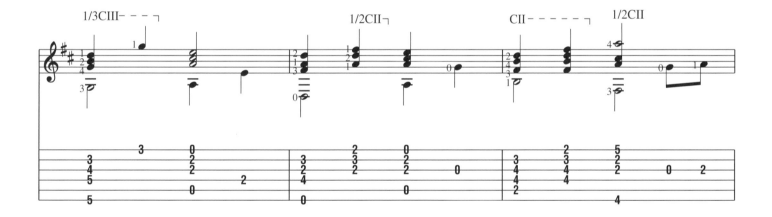

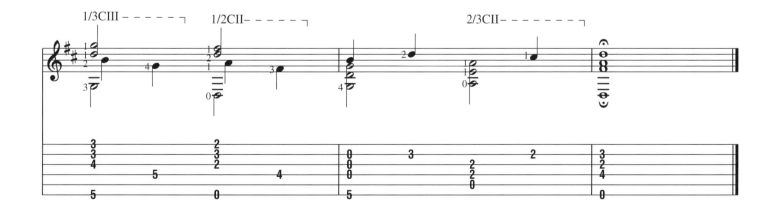

Deck the Hall

Traditional Welsh Carol

Moderately fast

The First Noël

17th Century English Carol
Music from W. Sandys' Christmas Carols

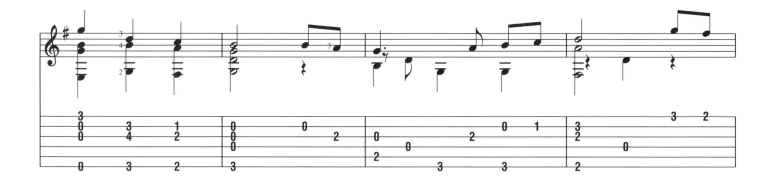

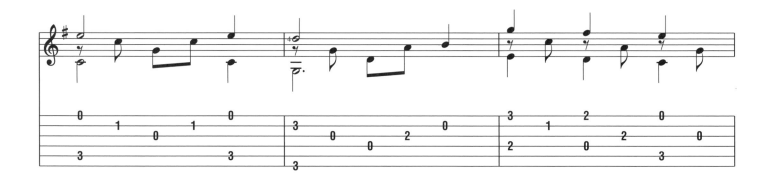

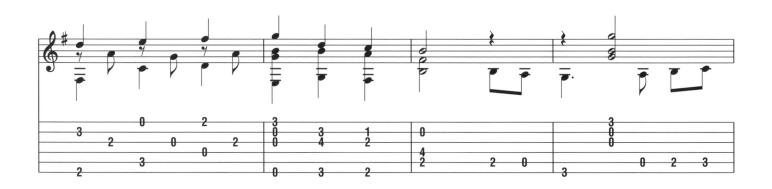

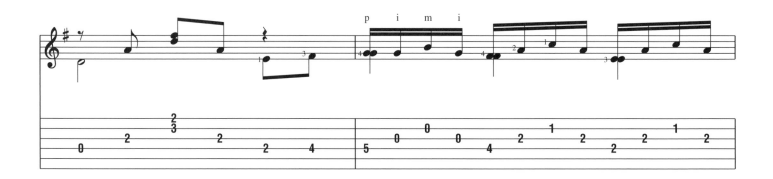

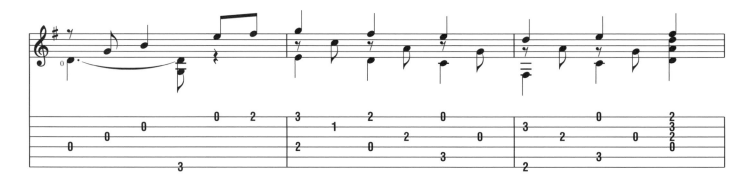

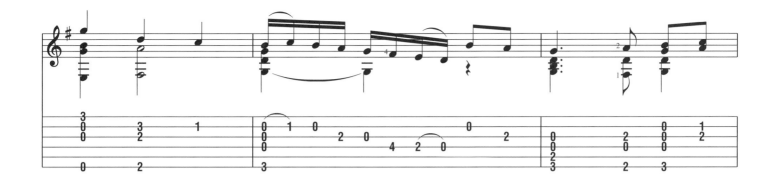

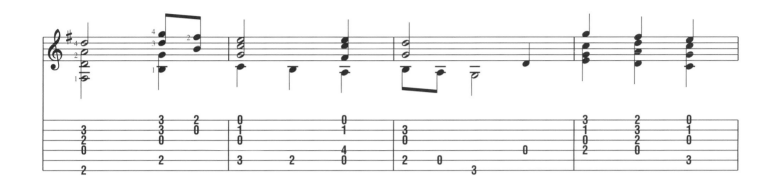

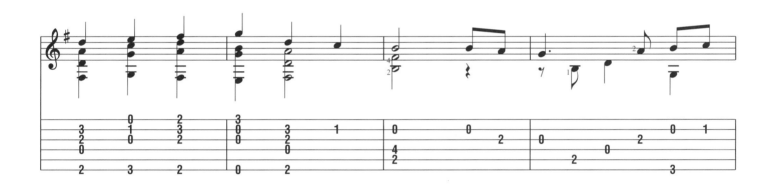

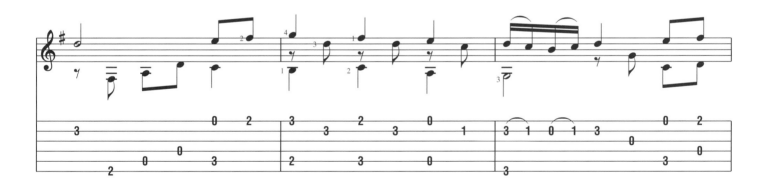

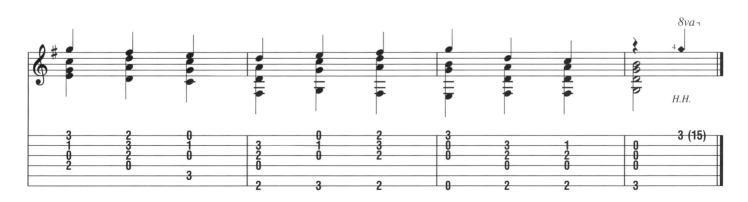

21

God Rest Ye Merry, Gentlemen

19th Century English Carol

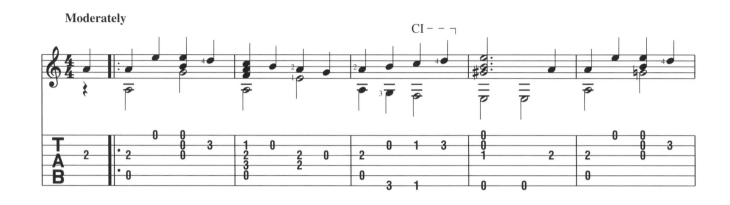

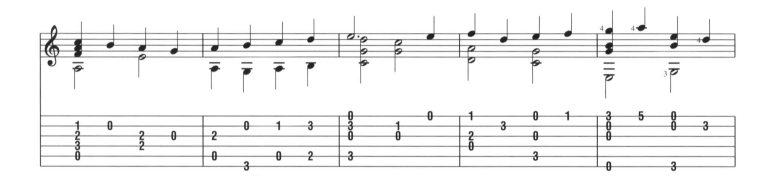

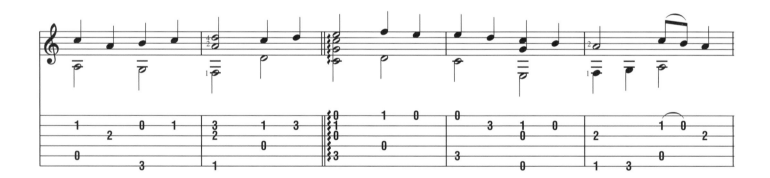

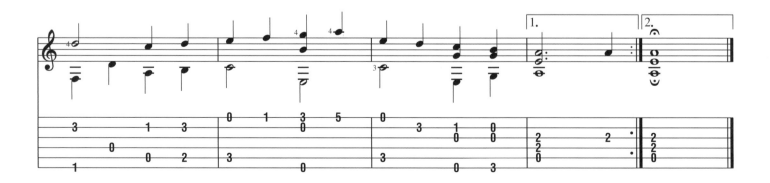

Good King Wenceslas

Music from Piae Cantiones

Drop D tuning:
(low to high) D–A–D–G–B–E

Moderately fast

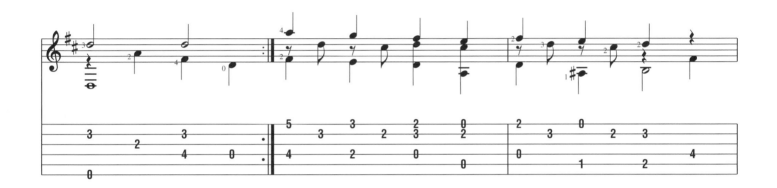

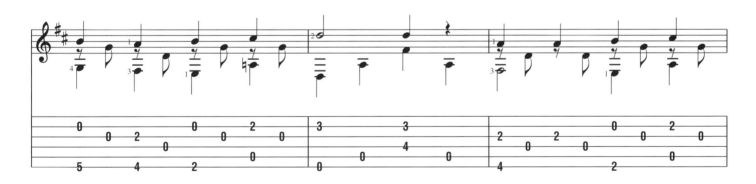

1/2 CII

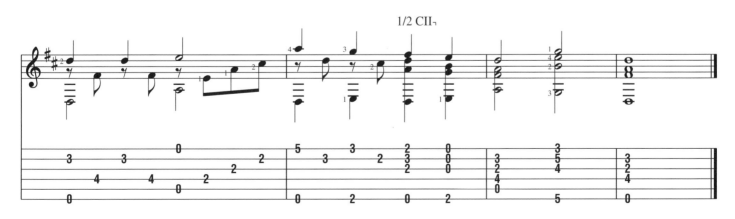

Hark! The Herald Angels Sing

Music by Felix Mendelssohn-Bartholdy

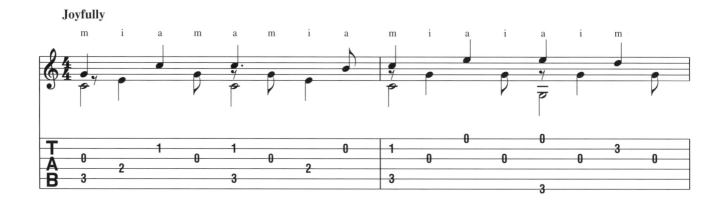

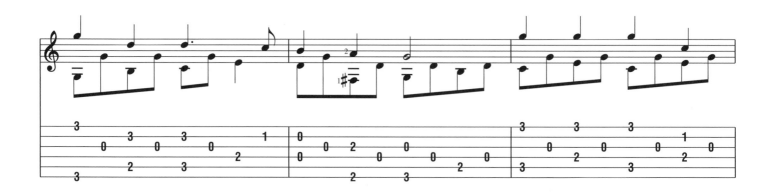

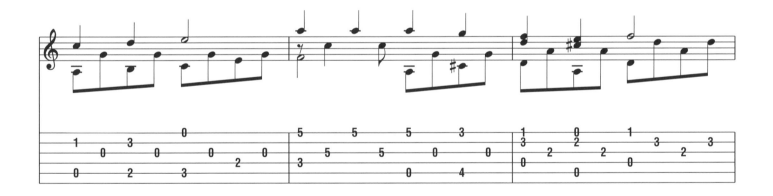

Here We Come A–Wassailing

Traditional

Moderately fast

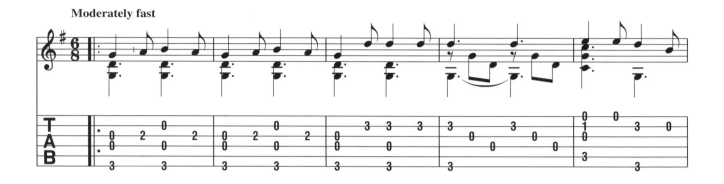

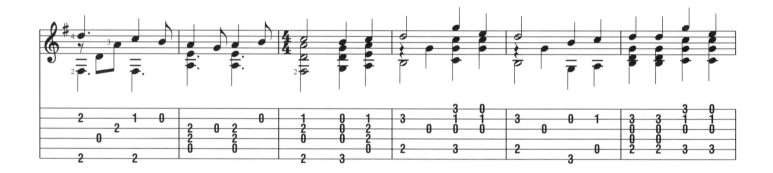

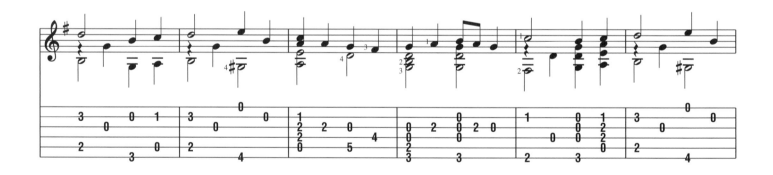

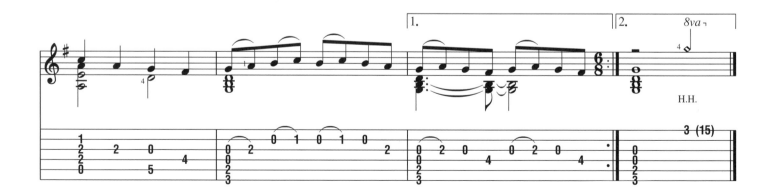

I Saw Three Ships

Traditional English Carol

Drop D tuning:
(low to high) D–A–D–G–B–E

Spirited

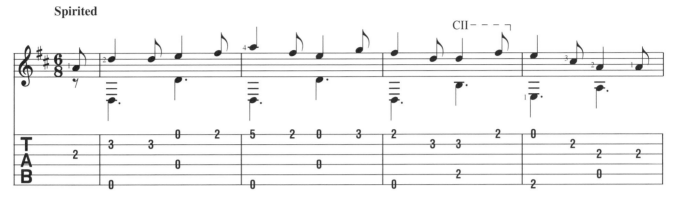

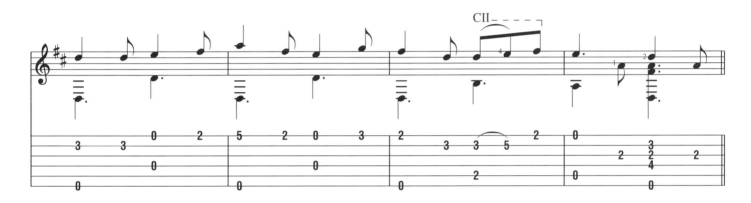

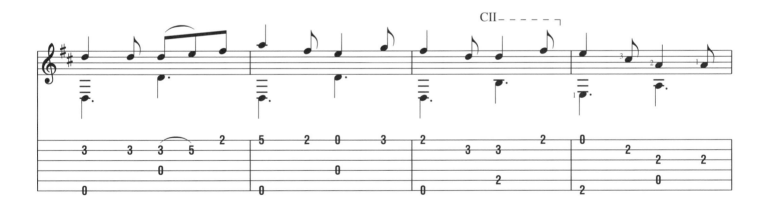

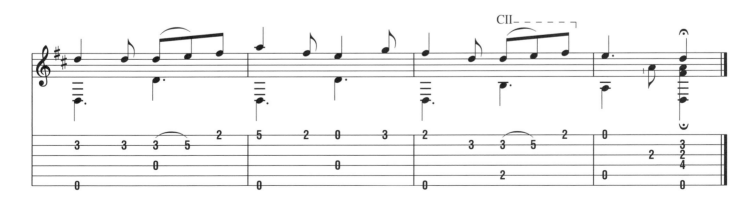

It Came Upon the Midnight Clear

Music by Richard Storrs WIllis

Drop D tuning:
(low to high) D–A–D–G–B–E

Moderately

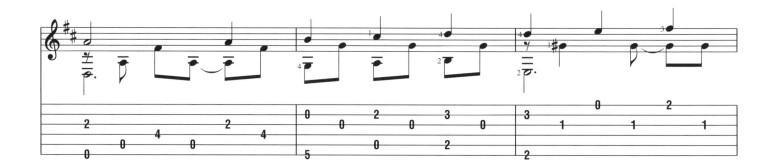

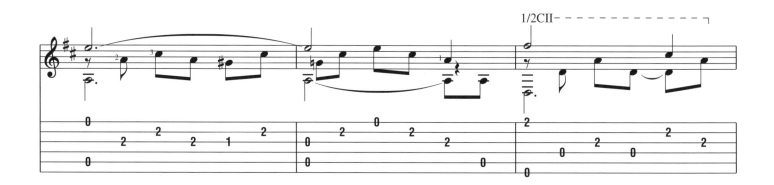

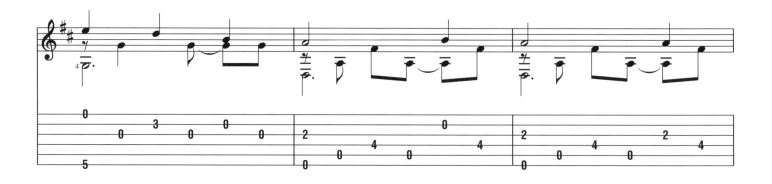

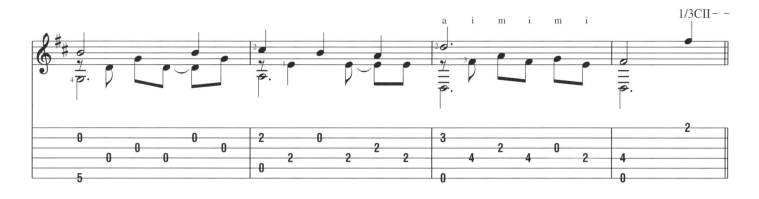

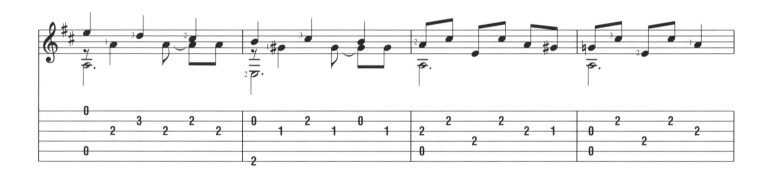

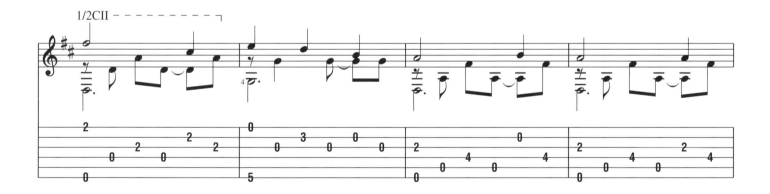

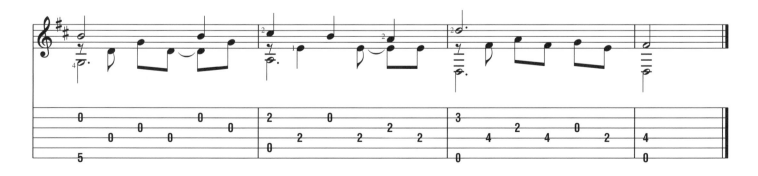

Jesu, Joy of Man's Desiring

By Johann Sebastian Bach

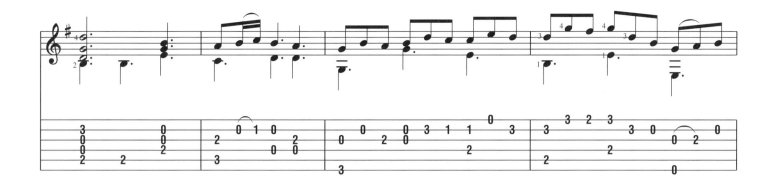

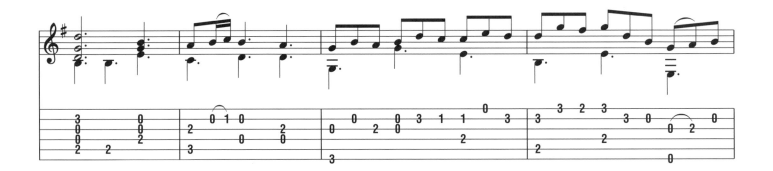

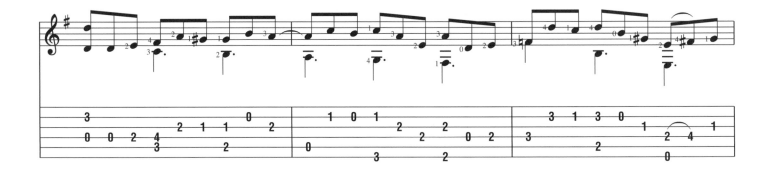

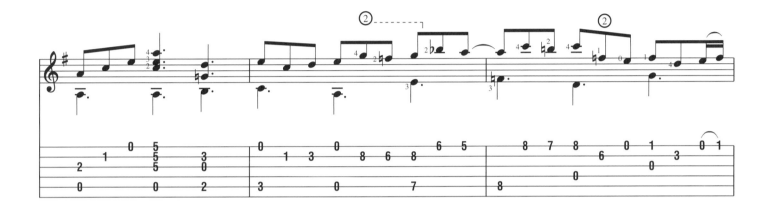

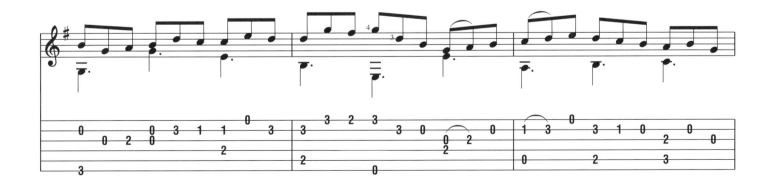

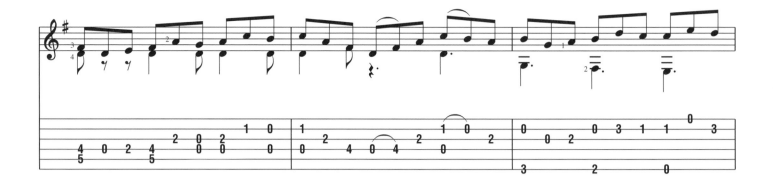

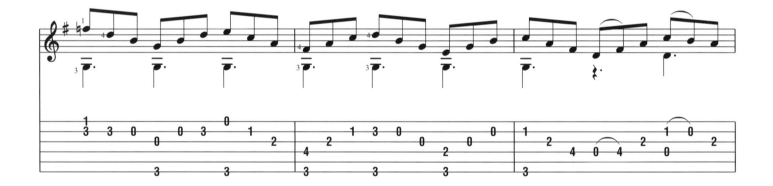

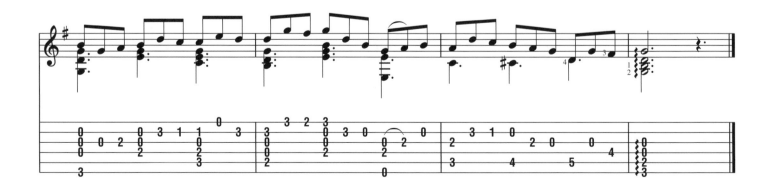

Joy to the World

Music by George Frideric Handel

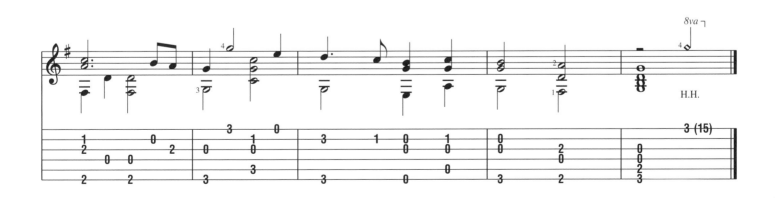

Jingle Bells

Words and Music by J. Pierpont

Brightly

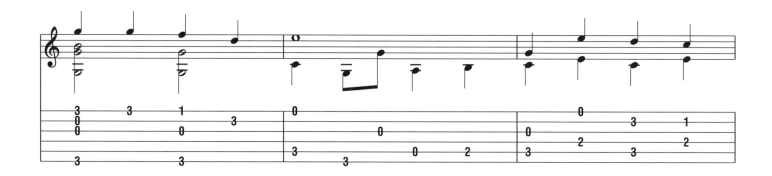

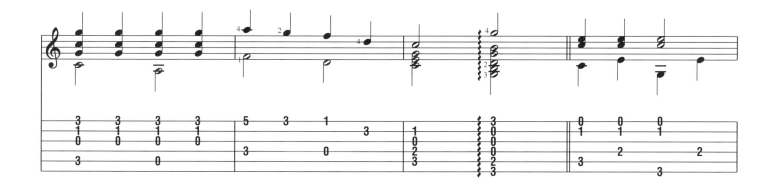

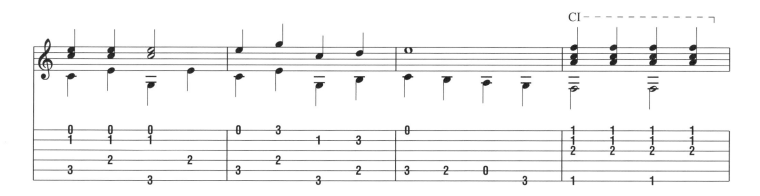

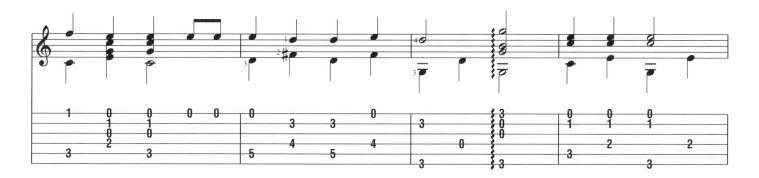

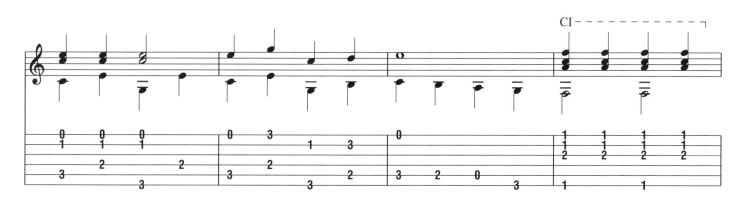

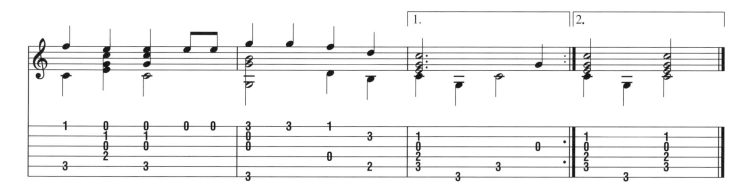

March

from The Nutcracker

by Pyotr Il'yich Tchaikovsky

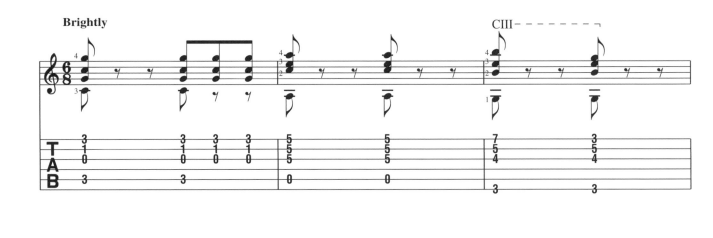

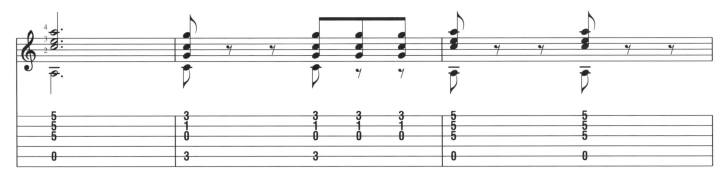

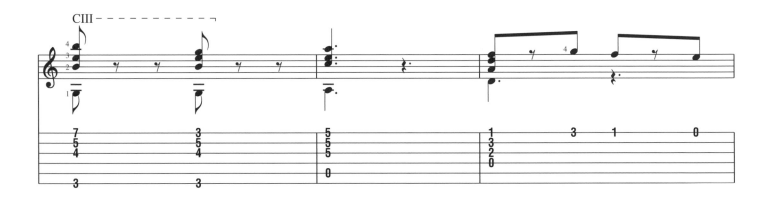

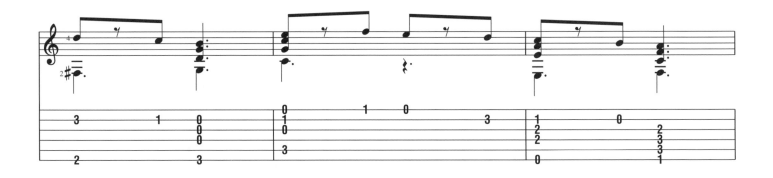

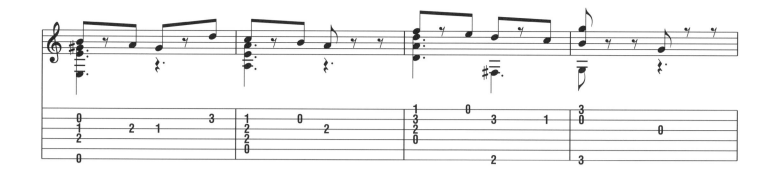

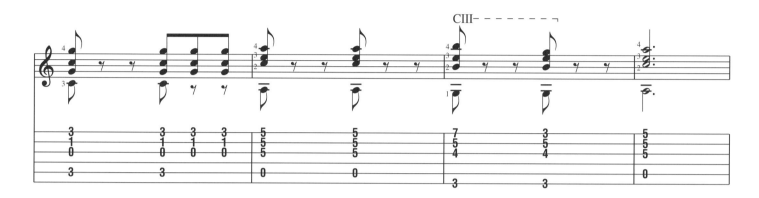

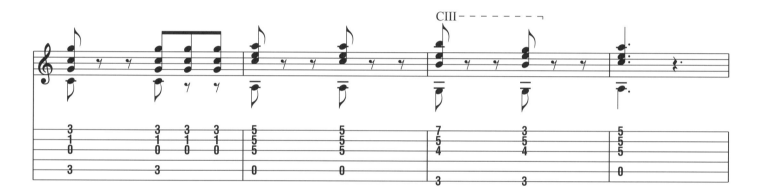

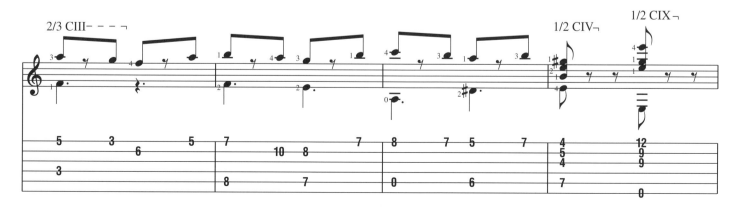

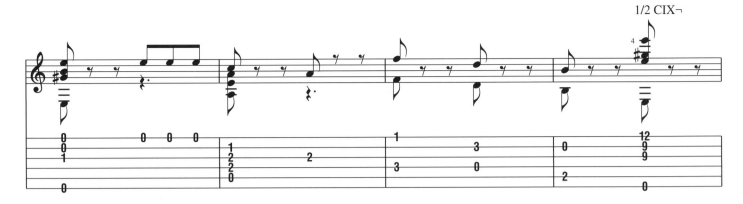

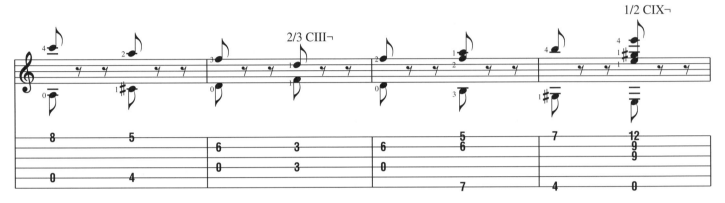

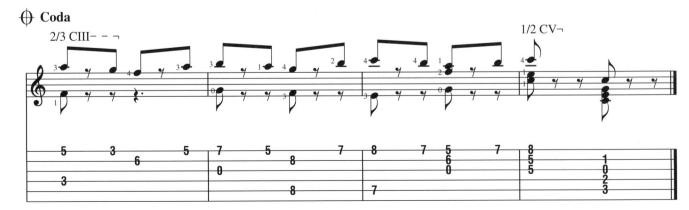

O Christmas Tree

Traditional German Carol

O Holy Night

Music by Adolphe Adam

Moderately slow

CVIII

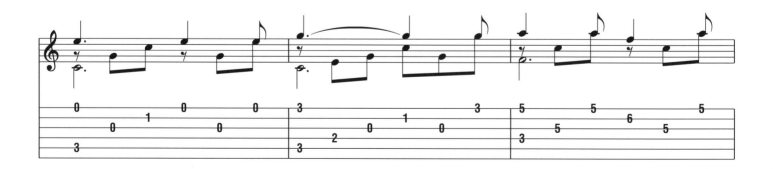

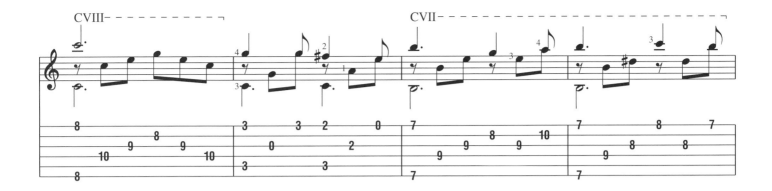

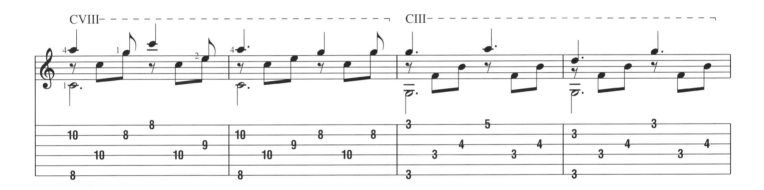

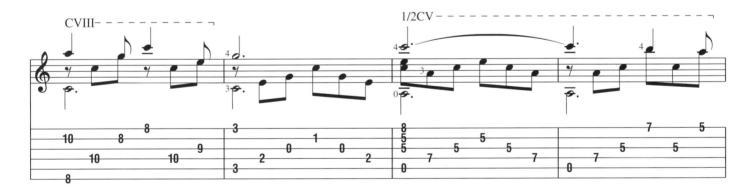

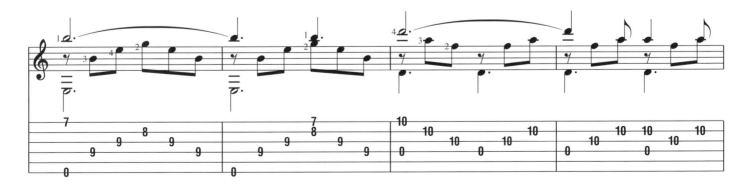

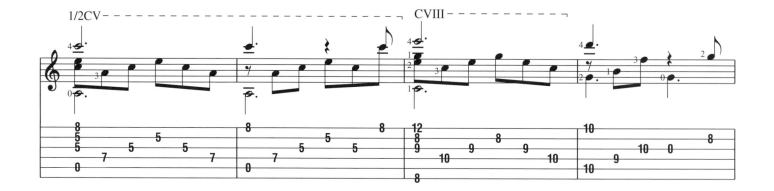

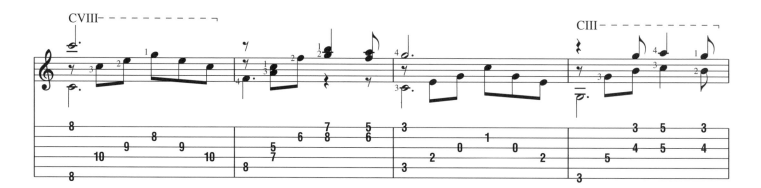

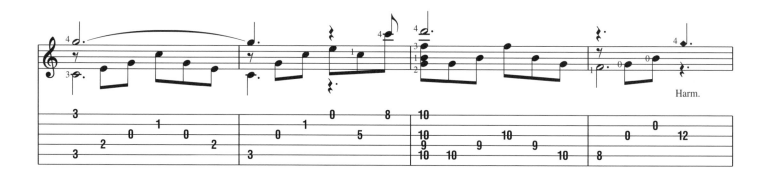

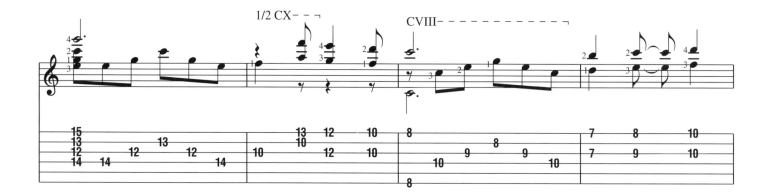

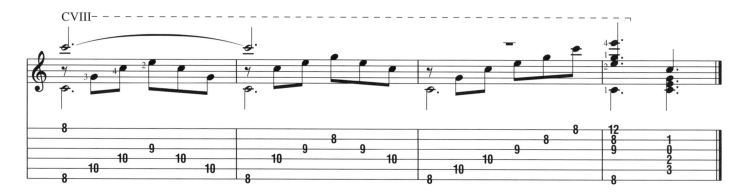

O Little Town of Bethlehem

Music by Lewis H. Redner

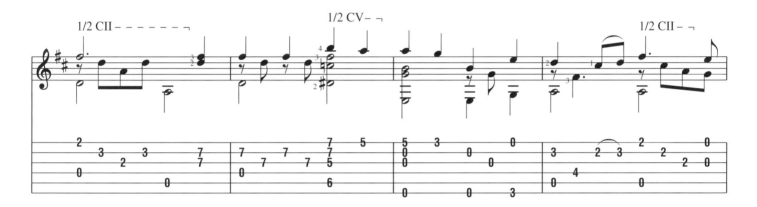

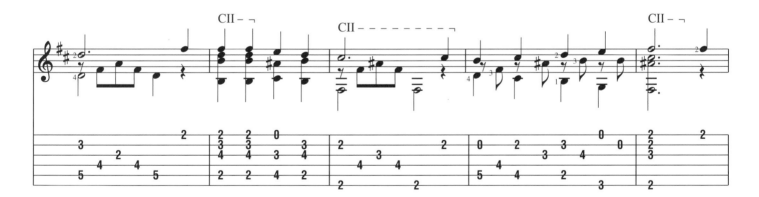

Sheep May Safely Graze

By Johann Sebastian Bach

Drop D tuning:
(low to high) D-A-D-G-B-E

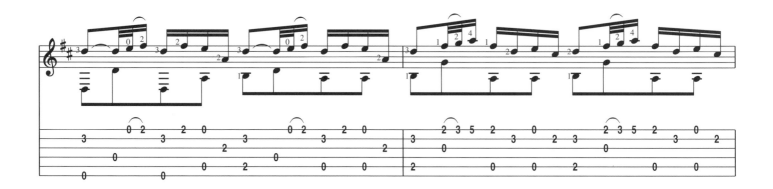

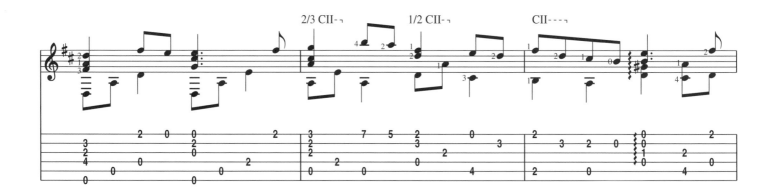

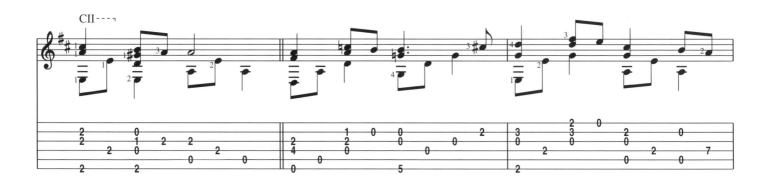

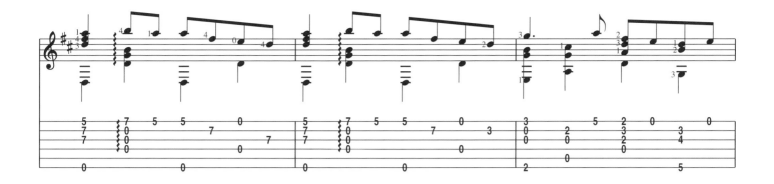

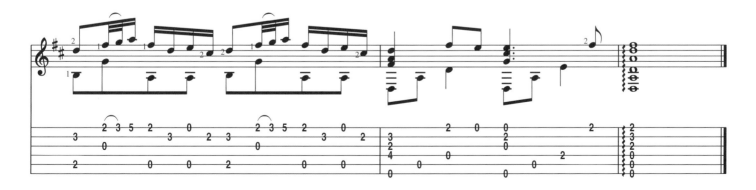

Silent Night

Music by Franz X. Gruber

Drop D tuning:
(low to high) D–A–D–G–B–E

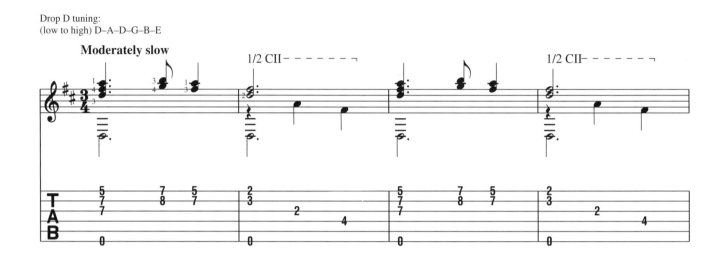

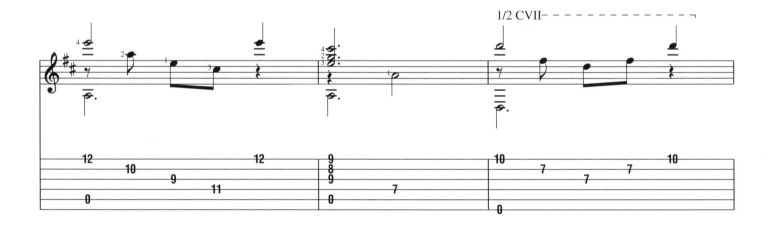

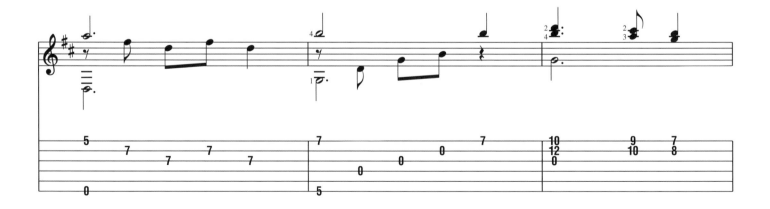

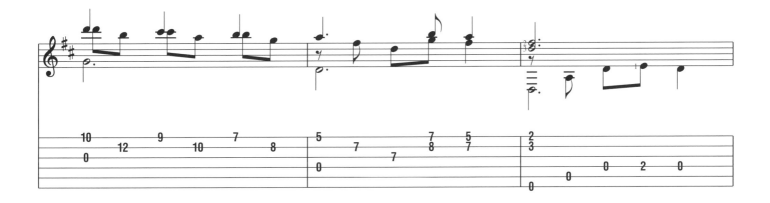

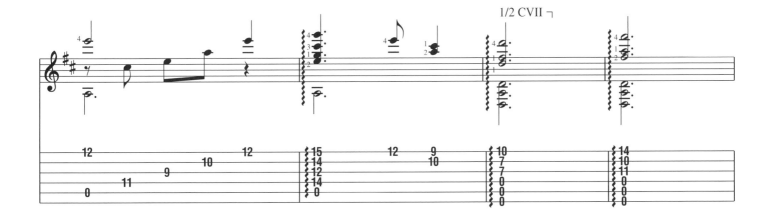

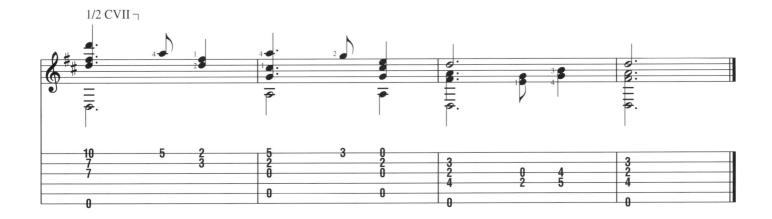

We Three Kings of Orient Are

Words and Music by John H. Hopkins, Jr.

Drop D tuning:
(low to high) D–A–D–G–B–E

Moderately

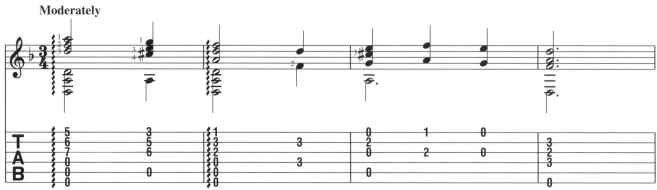

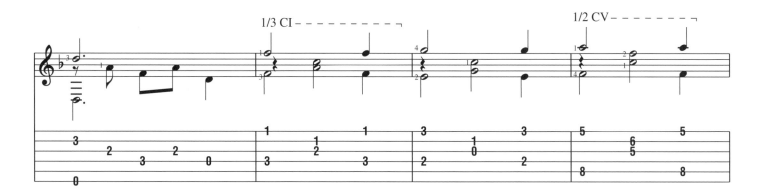

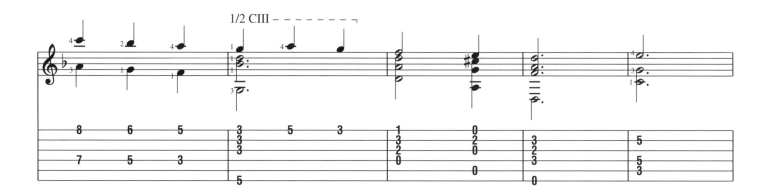

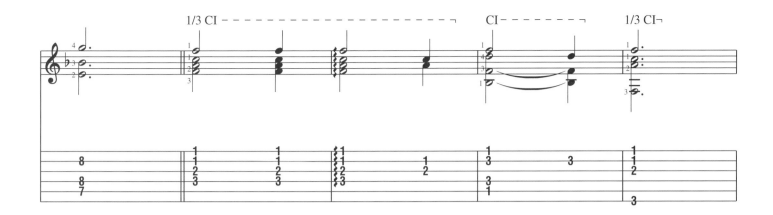

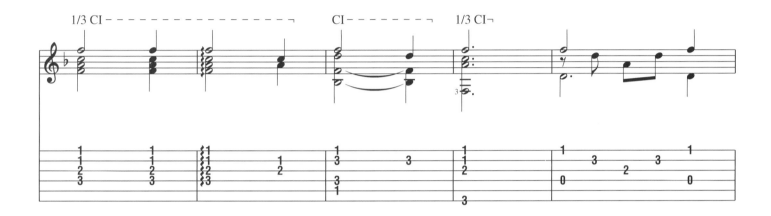

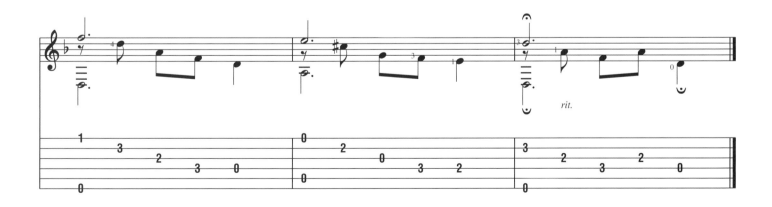

What Child Is This?

16th Century English Melody

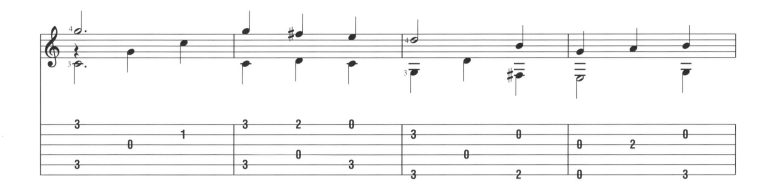

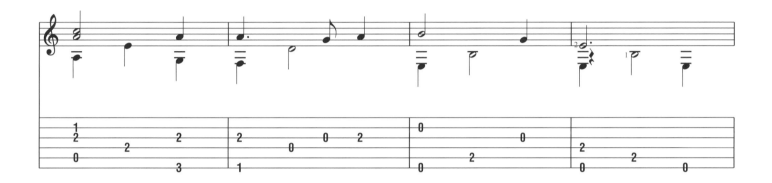

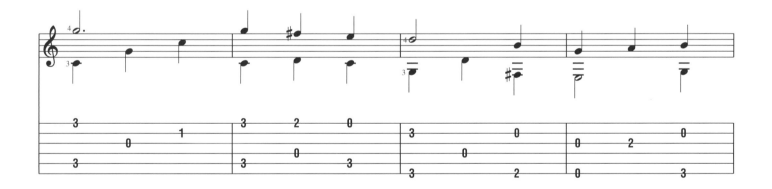

We Wish You a Merry Christmas

Traditional English Folksong

Moderately fast

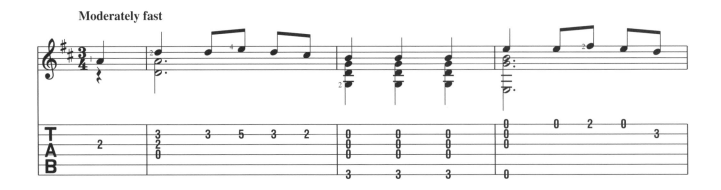

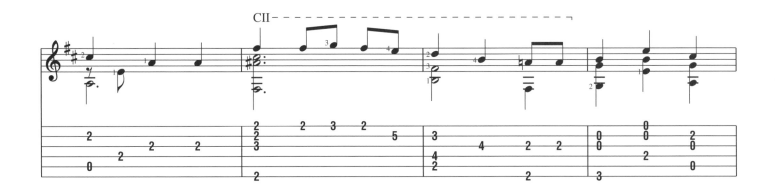

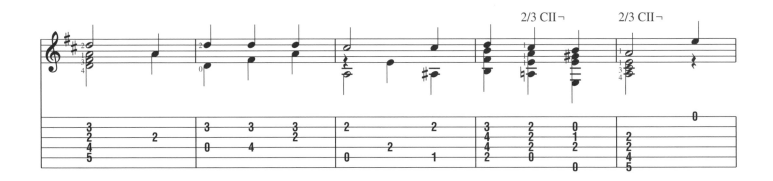

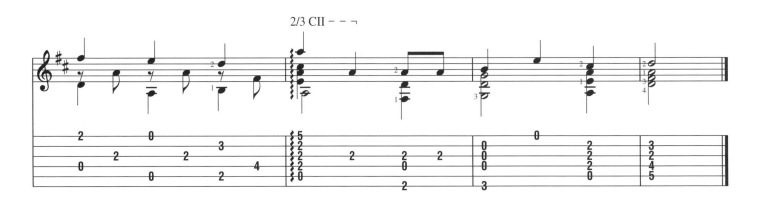

CLASSICAL GUITAR

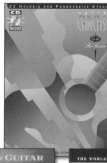

THE BEATLES FOR CLASSICAL GUITAR

Includes 20 solos from big Beatles hits arranged for classical guitar, complete with left-hand and right-hand fingering. Songs include: All My Loving • And I Love Her • Can't Buy Me Love • Fool on the Hill • From a Window • Hey Jude • If I Fell • Let It Be • Michelle • Norwegian Wood • Obla Di • Ticket to Ride • Yesterday • and more. Features arrangements and an introduction by Joe Washington, as well as his helpful hints on classical technique and detailed notes on how to play each song. The book also covers parts and specifications of the classical guitar, tuning, and Joe's "Strata System" – an easy-reading system applied to chord diagrams.

00699237 Classical Guitar $19.99

CZERNY FOR GUITAR

12 SCALE STUDIES FOR CLASSICAL GUITAR
by David Patterson

Adapted from Carl Czerny's *School of Velocity, Op. 299* for piano, this lesson book explores 12 keys with 12 different approaches or "treatments." You will explore a variety of articulations, ranges and technical perspectives as you learn each key. These arrangements will not only improve your ability to play scales fluently, but will also develop your ears, knowledge of the fingerboard, reading abilities, strength and endurance. In standard notation and tablature.

00701248 ....$9.99

MATTEO CARCASSI – 25 MELODIC AND PROGRESSIVE STUDIES, OP. 60

arr. Paul Henry

One of Carcassi's (1792-1853) most famous collections of classical guitar music – indispensable for the modern guitarist's musical and technical development. Performed by Paul Henry. 49-minute audio accompaniment.

00696506 Book/Online Audio $17.99

CLASSICAL & FINGERSTYLE GUITAR TECHNIQUES
INCLUDES TAB

by David Oakes • Musicians Institute

This Master Class is aimed at any electric or acoustic guitarist who wants a quick, thorough grounding in the essentials of classical and fingerstyle technique. Topics covered include: arpeggios and scales, free stroke and rest stroke, P-i scale technique, three-to-a-string patterns, natural and artificial harmonics, tremolo and rasgueado, and more. The book includes 12 intensive lessons for right and left hand in standard notation & tab, and the audio features 92 solo acoustic tracks.

00695171 Book/Online Audio $17.99

CLASSICAL GUITAR CHRISTMAS COLLECTION
INCLUDES TAB

Includes classical guitar arrangements in standard notation and tablature for more than two dozen beloved carols: Angels We Have Heard on High • Auld Lang Syne • Ave Maria • Away in a Manger • Canon in D • The First Noel • God Rest Ye Merry, Gentlemen • Hark! the Herald Angels Sing • I Saw Three Ships • Jesu, Joy of Man's Desiring • Joy to the World • O Christmas Tree • O Holy Night • Silent Night • What Child Is This? • and more.

00699493 Guitar Solo $10.99

CLASSICAL GUITAR WEDDING
INCLUDES TAB

Perfect for players hired to perform for someone's big day, this songbook features 16 classical wedding favorites arranged for solo guitar in standard notation and tablature. Includes: Air on the G String • Ave Maria • Bridal Chorus • Canon in D • Jesu, Joy of Man's Desiring • Minuet • Sheep May Safely Graze • Wedding March • and more.

00699563 Solo Guitar with Tab..............................$12.99

CLASSICAL MASTERPIECES FOR GUITAR
INCLUDES TAB

27 works by Bach, Beethoven, Handel, Mendelssohn, Mozart and more transcribed with standard notation and tablature. Now anyone can enjoy classical material regardless of their guitar background. Also features stay-open binding.

00699312 ....$14.99

MASTERWORKS FOR GUITAR
INCLUDES TAB

Over 60 Favorites from Four Centuries
World's Great Classical Music

Dozens of classical masterpieces: Allemande • Bourree • Canon in D • Jesu, Joy of Man's Desiring • Lagrima • Malaguena • Mazurka • Piano Sonata No. 14 in C# Minor (Moonlight) Op. 27 No. 2 First Movement Theme • Ode to Joy • Prelude No. I (Well-Tempered Clavier).

00699503 ....$19.99

HAL•LEONARD®

Visit Hal Leonard Online at **www.halleonard.com**

Prices, contents and availability subject to change without notice.

A MODERN APPROACH TO CLASSICAL GUITAR

by Charles Duncan

This multi-volume method was developed to allow students to study the art of classical guitar within a new, more contemporary framework. For private, class or self-instruction. Book One incorporates chord frames and symbols, as well as a recording to assist in tuning and to provide accompaniments for at-home practice. Book One also introduces beginning fingerboard technique and music theory. Book Two and Three build upon the techniques learned in Book One.

00695114 Book 1 – Book Only $6.99
00695113 Book 1 – Book/Online Audio.................$10.99
00695116 Book 2 – Book Only $6.99
00695115 Book 2 – Book/Online Audio.................$10.99
00699202 Book 3 – Book Only $9.99
00695117 Book 3 – Book/Online Audio.................$12.99
00695119 Composite Book/CD Pack $29.99

ANDRES SEGOVIA – 20 STUDIES FOR GUITAR

Sor/Segovia

20 studies for the classical guitar written by Beethoven's contemporary, Fernando Sor, revised, edited and fingered by the great classical guitarist Andres Segovia. These essential repertoire pieces continue to be used by teachers and students to build solid classical technique. Features 50-minute demonstration audio.

00695012 Book/Online Audio $19.99
00006363 Book Only..$7.99

THE FRANCISCO COLLECTION TÁRREGA
INCLUDES TAB

edited and performed by Paul Henry

Considered the father of modern classical guitar, Francisco Tárrega revolutionized guitar technique and composed a wealth of music that will be a cornerstone of classical guitar repertoire for centuries to come. This unique book/audio pack features 14 of his most outstanding pieces in standard notation and tab, edited and performed by virtuoso Paul Henry. Includes: Adelita • Capricho Árabe • Estudio Brillante • Grand Jota • Lágrima • Malagueña • María • Recuerdos de la Alhambra • Tango • and more, plus bios of Tárrega and Henry.

00698993 Book/Online Audio $19.99

THE PUBLICATIONS OF
CHRISTOPHER PARKENING

CHRISTOPHER PARKENING – DUETS AND CONCERTOS

Throughout his career, Christopher Parkening has had the opportunity to perform with many of the world's leading artists and orchestras, and this folio contains many selections from those collaborations. All of the pieces included here have been edited and fingered for the guitar by Christopher Parkening himself.

00690938..$24.99

THE CHRISTOPHER PARKENING GUITAR METHOD, VOL. 1 – REVISED

in collaboration with
Jack Marshall and David Brandon

Learn the art of the classical guitar with this premier method for beginners by one of the world's preeminent virtuosos and the recognized heir to the legacy of Andrés Segovia. Learn basic classical guitar technique by playing beautiful pieces of music, including over 50 classical pieces, 26 exercises, and 14 duets. Includes notes in the first position, how to hold the guitar, tuning, right and left hand technique, arpeggios, tone production, placement of fingers and nails, flats, naturals, key signatures, the bar, and more. Also includes many helpful photos and illustrations, plus sections on the history of the classical guitar, selecting a guitar, guitar care, and more.

00695228 Book...$12.99
00696023 Book/Online Audio $19.99

THE CHRISTOPHER PARKENING GUITAR METHOD, VOL. 2

Intermediate to Upper-Intermediate Level

Continues where Vol. 1 leaves off. Teaches: all notes in the upper position; tone production; advanced techniques such as tremolo, harmonics, vibrato, pizzicato and slurs; practice tips; stylistic interpretation; and more. The first half of the book deals primarily with technique, while the second half of the book applies the technique with repertoire pieces. As a special bonus, this book includes 32 previously unpublished Parkening edition pieces by composers including Dowland, Bach, Scarlatti, Sor, Tarrega and other, plus three duets for two guitars.

00695229 Book...$12.99
00696024 Book/Online Audio $19.99

PARKENING AND THE GUITAR – VOL. 1

Music of Two Centuries:
Popular New Transcriptions for Guitar
Virtuoso Music for Guitar

Ten transcriptions for solo guitar of beautiful music from many periods and styles, edited and fingered by Christopher Parkening. All pieces are suitable for performance by the advanced guitarist. Ten selections: Afro-Cuban Lullaby • Empress of the Pagodes (Ravel) • Menuet (Ravel) • Minuet in D (Handel) • Passacaille (Weiss) • Pastourelle (Poulenc) • Pavane for a Dead Princess (Ravel) • Pavane for a Sleeping Beauty (Ravel) • Preambulo (Scarlatti-Ponce) • Sarabande (Handel).

00699105..$9.95

PARKENING AND THE GUITAR – VOL. 2

Music of Two Centuries:
Popular New Transcriptions for Guitar
Virtuoso Music for Guitar

Nine more selections for the advanced guitarist: Clair de Lune (Debussy) • Giga (Visée) • The Girl with the Flaxen Hair (Debussy) • Gymnopedie Nos. I-III (Satie) • The Little Shepherd (Debussy) • The Mysterious Barricades (Couperin) • Sarabande (Debussy).

00699106..$9.95

CHRISTOPHER PARKENING – ROMANZA

Virtuoso Music for Guitar

Three wonderful transcriptions edited and fingered by Parkening: Catalonian Song • Rumores de la Caleta • Romance.

00699103..$9.99

CHRISTOPHER PARKENING – SACRED MUSIC FOR THE GUITAR, VOL. 1

Seven inspirational arrangements, transcriptions and compositions covering traditional Christian melodies from several centuries. These selections appear on the Parkening album Sacred Music for the Guitar. Includes: Präludium (Bach) • Our Great Savior • God of Grace and God of Glory (2 guitars) • Brethren, We Have Met to Worship • Deep River • Jesus, We Want to Meet • Evening Prayer.

00699095..$12.99

CHRISTOPHER PARKENING – SACRED MUSIC FOR THE GUITAR, VOL. 2

Seven more selections from the album *Sacred Music for the Guitar:* Hymn of Christian Joy (guitar and harpsichord) • Simple Gifts • Fairest Lord Jesus • Stir Thy Church, O God Our Father • All Creatures of Our God and King • Glorious Things of Thee Are Spoken • Praise Ye the Lord (2 guitars).

00699100..$12.99

CHRISTOPHER PARKENING – SOLO PIECES

Sixteen transcriptions for solo guitar edited and fingered by Parkening, including: Allegro • Danza • Fugue • Galliard • I Stand at the Threshold • Prelude • Sonata in D • Suite Española • Suite in D Minor • and more.

00690939..$19.99

PARKENING PLAYS BACH

Virtuoso Music for Guitar

Nine transcriptions edited and fingered by Parkening: Preludes I, VI & IX • Gavottes I & II • Jesu, Joy of Man's Desiring • Sheep May Safely Graze • Wachet Auf, Ruft Uns Die Stemme • Be Thou with Me • Sleepers Awake (2 guitars).

00699104..$9.95

CHRISTOPHER PARKENING – VIRTUOSO PERFORMANCES

DVD

This DVD features performances and career highlights from classical guitar virtuoso Christopher Parkening (filmed in 1971, 1973, 1998 and 2003). Viewers can watch feature titles in their entirety or select individual songs. As a bonus, there is archival footage of Andrés Segovia performing in studio, circa 1950. The DVD also includes an informational booklet. 95 minutes.

00320506 DVD $24.99

HAL•LEONARD®

www.halleonard.com

Prices, contents and availability subject to change without notice.